IN THIS ISSUE:

I0478826

tourism.com
TATTLER
ISSUE 11 NOVEMBER 2016

PUBLISHER
Tourism Tattler (Pty) Ltd.
PO Box 891, Umhlanga Rocks, 4320
KwaZulu-Natal, South Africa.
Website: www.tourismtattler.com

EXECUTIVE EDITOR Des Langkilde
Cell: +27 (0)82 374 7260
Fax: +27 (0)86 651 8080
E-mail: editor@tourismtattler.com
Skype: tourismtattler

MAGAZINE ADVERTISING
ADVERTISING DIRECTOR Bev Langkilde
Cell: +27 (0)71 224 9971
Fax: +27 (0)86 656 3860
E-mail: bev@tourismtattler.com
Skype: bevtourismtattler

SUBSCRIPTIONS
http://eepurl.com/bocldD

BACK ISSUES (Click on the covers below)..

▼ OCT 2016	▼ SEP 2016	▼ AUG 2016

▼ JUL 2016	▼ JUN 2016	▼ MAY 2016

▼ APR 2016	▼ MAR 2016	▼ FEB 2016

▼ JAN 2016	▼ DEC 2015	▼ NOV 2015

CONTENTS

EDITORIAL CONTRIBUTORS

Adam Jacot de Boinod
Adv. Louis Nel
Debbie Cooper
Kagiso Mosue
Martin Janse van Vuuren

Mary Smith
Paul W. Reynell
Rut Gomez Sobrino
Thandiwe Mathibela
Vernon Wait

MAGAZINE SPONSORS

ACCREDITATION

Official Travel Trade Journal and Media Partner to:

The Africa Travel Association (ATA)

Tel: +1 212 447 1357 • Email: info@africatravelassociation.org • Website: www.africatravelassociation.org

ATA is a division of the Corporate Council on Africa (CCA), and a registered non-profit trade association in the USA, with headquarters in Washington, DC and chapters around the world. ATA is dedicated to promoting travel and tourism to Africa and strengthening intra-Africa partnerships. Established in 1975, ATA provides services to both the public and private sectors of the industry.

The African Travel & Tourism Association (Atta)

Tel: +44 20 7937 4408 • Email: info@atta.travel • Website: www.atta.travel

Members in 22 African countries and 37 worldwide use Atta to: Network and collaborate with peers in African tourism; Grow their online presence with a branded profile; Ask and answer specialist questions and give advice; and Attend key industry events.

National Accommodation Association of South Africa (NAA-SA)

Tel: +27 86 186 2272 • Fax: +2786 225 9858 • Website: www.naa-sa.co.za

The NAA-SA is a network of mainly smaller accommodation providers around South Africa – from B&Bs in country towns offering comfortable personal service to luxurious boutique city lodges with those extra special touches – you're sure to find a suitable place, and at the same time feel confident that your stay at an NAA-SA member's establishment will meet your requirements.

Regional Tourism Organisation of Southern Africa (RETOSA)

Tel: +27 11 315 2420/1 • Fax: +27 11 315 2422 • Website: www.retosa.co.za

RETOSA is a Southern African Development Community (SADC) institution responsible for tourism growth and development. RETOSA's aims are to increase tourist arrivals to the region through. RETOSA Member States are Angola, Botswana, DR Congo, Lesotho, Madagascar, Malawi, Mauritius, Mozambique, Namibia, Seychelles, South Africa, Swaziland, Tanzania, Zambia and Zimbabwe.

Southern African Vehicle Rental and Leasing Association (SAVRALA)

Contact: manager@savrala.co.za • Website: www.savrala.co.za

Founded in the 1970's, SAVRALA is the representative voice of Southern Africa's vehicle rental, leasing and fleet management sector. Our members have a combined national footprint with more than 600 branches countrywide. SAVRALA are instrumental in steering industry standards and continuously strive to protect both their members' interests, and those of the public, and are therefore widely respected within corporate and government sectors.

Seychelles Hospitality & Tourism Association (SHTA)

Tel: +248 432 5560 • Fax: +248 422 5718 • Website: www.shta.sc

The Seychelles Hospitality and Tourism Association was created in 2002 when the Seychelles Hotel Association merged with the Seychelles Hotel and Guesthouse Association. SHTA's primary focus is to unite all Seychelles tourism industry stakeholders under one association in order to be better prepared to defend the interest of the industry and its sustainability as the pillar of the country's economy.

Tourism, Hotel Investment and Networking Conference 2016

Website: www.thincafrica.hvsconferences.com

THINC Africa 2016 takes place in Cape Town from 6-7 September.

International Coalition of Tourism Partners (ICTP)

Website: www.tourismpartners.org

ICTP is a travel and tourism coalition of global destinations committed to Quality Services and Green Growth.

International Institute for Peace through Tourism

Website: www.iipt.org

IIPT is dedicated to fostering tourism initiatives that contribute to international understanding and cooperation.

World Travel Market

WTM Africa - Cape Town in April, WTM Latin America - São Paulo in April, and WTM - London in November. WTM is the place to do business.

The Safari Awards

Website: www.safariawards.com

Safari Award finalists are amongst the top 3% in Africa and the winners are unquestionably the best.

World Luxury Hotel Awards

Website: www.luxuryhotelawards.com

World Luxury Hotel Awards is an international company that provides award recognition to the best hotels from all over the world.

7 - 9 Nov 2016

Discover the world

£2.5 Billion*
of new business

5,000**
exhibitors
from across the world

49,273**
attendees
from 182 countries

Official Media Partner

Discounted Travel
Please visit
wtmlondon.com/discounts

Register now
wtmlondon.com

29 OCTOBER 2016

10 Years

WORLD LUXURY HOTEL
AWARDS

EST. 2006

THIS YEAR, THE WORLD LUXURY HOTEL AWARDS IS CELEBRATING A DECADE OF HOTELIERING EXCELLENCE AT THE ST. REGIS DOHA, QATAR. THIS EXTRAORDINARY CELEBRATION WILL HONOUR THE CRÈME DE LA CRÈME OF THE LUXURY HOSPITALITY INDUSTRY BY AWARDING LUXURY HOTELS FROM ACROSS THE WORLD FOR OUTSTANDING ACHIEVEMENT ON A GLOBAL PLATFORM.

HOSTED AT

ST REGIS
DOHA

OFFICIAL PARTNER

FRANCE 24

FOR MORE INFO, VISIT WWW.LUXURYHOTELAWARDS.COM

A night with the STARS

It was a night of honour and glamour when the South African tourism industry celebrated its top business owners and service providers at the fourth annual Lilizela Tourism Awards on 16 October 2016.

By **Thandiwe Mathibela**

Joined by various key industry players, South Africa's Minister of Tourism, Mr Derek Hanekom, also announced the 2016 Minister's Award at the star-studded gala event held at the Sandton Convention Centre in Johannesburg.

This prestigious award, which recognises tourism innovators and pioneers, went to renowned Mpumalanga artist, Esther Mahlangu. A previous Lilizela category winner in the Roots and Culture category, Mahlangu's colourful Ndebele designs have been exhibited around the world and have graced global brands such as BMW, British Airways, Fiat and Belvedere luxury vodka, placing South African traditional art and design on the international map.

The 80-year-old Mahlangu joined 53 other national winners of the Lilizela Tourism Awards, who travellers had voted the best of the best in categories ranging from service excellence and entrepreneurship to sustainable development (*see the complete list on pages 06 and 07*).

"The Lilizela Tourism Awards give us the opportunity to celebrate trailblazers such as Mam' Esther, as well as service excellence in the South African tourism industry in general. Tonight is an opportunity to pause and thank these individuals and businesses for their contribution to putting South Africa firmly on the global stage by ensuring their product and service offerings are of the highest standard," said Minister Hanekom.

"With 5.8 million people having come to South Africa between January and July this year, the number of tourists is on the rise. By being service–oriented, the businesses celebrated today help to ensure that this growth path continues, guaranteeing memorable experiences for all tourists," he added.

The 2016 Lilizela Tourism Awards, an initiative of the National Department of Tourism and spearheaded by South African Tourism, was a star-studded celebratory affair, which gave players and stakeholders in the country's tourism industry the opportunity to come together to toast to excellence and be inspired by the example of others.

The awards were established in 2013 to recognise and reward exemplary service among businesses in the local tourism sector, ranging from accommodation establishments and tour operators to scenic attractions and cultural heritage sites.

In 2016, the awards attracted a record number of 1122 entries, up 18% from last year's total. Tourism businesses across the nine provinces were encouraged to enter, with a call that they be graded with the Tourism Grading Council of South Africa, a unit of South African Tourism.

Members of the public were then invited to have their say on the Lilizela Tourism Awards website by voting. These votes together with those from various platforms such as TripAdvisor and TGCSA's Tourism Analytics Programme, formed 80% of the score for each entry. A panel of high-level judges for each category, drawn from the industry and academia, contributed the remaining 20% of each establishment's score.

From these calculations, 589 finalists were selected nationwide, and each province held its own awards ceremony in the run-up to the national finals. During these provincial award ceremonies, 262 provincial winners were celebrated.

This provincial shortlist was further narrowed down to 53 national winners, who were honoured with trophies on Sunday night. Of the national Lilizela winners, most are from the Western Cape (17), followed by the Eastern Cape with 10.

Entry to the Lilizela Tourism Awards is free and tourism businesses of all sizes are encouraged to enter in a bid to help develop, grow and transform the industry. 🆃

Entries for the 2017 Lilizela Awards open on 1 December 2016. Visit www.lilizela.co.za.

About the Author: Thandiwe Mathibela is the Communications Manager at South African Tourism. www.southafrica.net

Winner of the 2016 Minister's Award, renowned Mpumalanga artist, Esther Mahlangu.

HONOURING THE BEST OF THE BEST

THE LILIZELA TOURISM AWARDS 2016

PRESENTING ALL 2016 WINNERS

ACCOMMODATION AWARDS

EASTERN CAPE

Name	CATEGORY	
Amapondo Backpackers	Backpacking & Hosteling 2-Star	(N)
Island Vibe Jeffreys Bay	Backpacking & Hosteling 4-Star	
Tube 'n Axe Backpackers Lodge	Backpacking & Hosteling 3-Star	(N)
Benri B&B	Bed & Breakfast 4-Star	
Lemon Tree Lane Bed and Breakfast	Bed & Breakfast 5-Star	(N)
River Road Guest House	Bed & Breakfast 3-Star	
Dwesa Nature Reserve	Caravan & Camping 3-Star	
Comfrey Cottage	Country House 4-Star	
Ganora Guest Farm & Excursions	Country House 3-Star	
Tenahead Mountain Lodge & Reserve	Country House 5-Star	
Bayethe Tented Lodge Shamwari	Game Lodge 5-Star	
Harmony Game Lodge	Game Lodge 3-Star	
Hlosi Game Lodge	Game Lodge 4-Star	
Forest Hall Guest House	Guest House 4-Star	
Hacklewood Hill Country House	Guest House 5-Star	
Victoria Manor	Guest House 3-Star	
MyPond Hotel	Hotel 4-Star	
Prana Lodge	Hotel 5-Star	
Road Lodge Port Elizabeth Airport	Hotel 2-Star	
Royal Courtyard	Hotel 3-Star	
Town Lodge Port Elizabeth	Hotel 2-Star	(N)
Miarestate Hotel & Spa	Lodge 5-Star	
Misty Mountain Reserve	Lodge 4-Star	
The Boardwalk Hotel	MESE* 5-Star	
Mansfield Private Game Reserve	Self Catering Exclusive 3-Star	
Seashells Luxury Accommodation	Self Catering Exclusive 4-Star	
The Oyster Box Beach House	Self Catering Exclusive 5-Star	
Beach Break	Self Catering Shared 5-Star	(N)
Cape St Francis Resort - Club Break	Self Catering Shared 2-Star	
Thunzi Bush Lodge	Self Catering Shared 4-Star	

FREE STATE

Name	CATEGORY	
Lions Rest Country Estate	Country House 3-Star	
Gariep, A Forever Resort (Camping)	Caravan & Camping 3-Star	09
Kamohelong Luxury Accommodation	Bed & Breakfast 3-Star	
Art Lovers Guesthouse	Guest House 5-Star	
Castello Guest House Bloemfontein	Guest House 4-Star	
Rochilla Guesthouse	Guest House 3-Star	
Anta Boga Hotel	Hotel 5-Star	
Golden Gate Hotel & Chalets	Hotel 3-Star	
Letsatsi Game Lodge	Lodge 4-Star	
Lionsrock Lodge	Lodge 5-Star	
Wild Horses Lodge	Lodge 5-Star	
Mont d' Or Hotel	MESE* 4-Star	
Gariep, A Forever Resort (Conference)	MESE* 3-Star	09
Golden Gate NP Highlands Mountain Retreat	Self Catering Exclusive 3-Star	
Gariep, A Forever Resort (Chalets)	Self Catering Shared 3-Star	09 (N)

GAUTENG

Name	CATEGORY	
Curiocity Backpackers	Backpacking & Hosteling 4-Star	(N)
Naledi Backpackers	Backpacking & Hosteling 2-Star	
Terrylin Backpackers	Backpacking & Hosteling 4-Star	
Abbotsford House	Bed & Breakfast 3-Star	
Hyde Park Villas	Bed & Breakfast 4-Star	
Sherewood Lodge	Bed & Breakfast 4-Star	
Oxbow Country Estate	Country House 4-Star	
Villa Amor	Country House 5-Star	
Flamingo's Nest Guest House & Conf Centre	Guest House 3-Star	(N)
Liz at Lancaster Guesthouse	Guest House 4-Star	
Opikopi Guest House	Guest House 5-Star	
Peermont Metcourt	Hotel 3-Star	
Road Lodge Southgate	Hotel 2-Star	
Thaba Eco Hotel	Hotel 4-Star	(N)
The View Boutique Hotel	Hotel 5-Star	
Town Lodge Johannesburg Airport	Hotel 2-Star	
The Forum / The Campus	MESE* 5-Star	
Oxbow Country Estate	MESE* 4-Star	
Blue Roan Country Lodge	Self Catering Exclusive 4-Star	
Nullarbor Cottages	Self Catering Exclusive 3-Star	

KWAZULU-NATAL

Name	CATEGORY	
Happy Hippo Accommodation	Backpacking & Hosteling 3-Star	
Azalea Bed and Breakfast	Bed & Breakfast 3-Star	
St Lucia Wetlands Guest House	Bed & Breakfast 4-Star	
Westville Bed & Breakfast	Bed & Breakfast 5-Star	
ATKV Drakensville Holiday Resort	Caravan & Camping 3-Star	
ATKV Natalia Beach Resort	Caravan & Camping 4-Star	
Days at Sea	Country House 5-Star	
Lythwood Lodge	Country House 4-Star	
Amakhosi Safari Lodge	Game Lodge 5-Star	
Leopard Mountain	Game Lodge 4-Star	(N)
Rain Farm Game and Lodge	Game Lodge 3-Star	
Ammazulu African Palace	Guest House 5-Star	
Elegant Lodge Pongola	Guest House 4-Star	
Lodge Afrique	Guest House 4-Star	
Drakensberg Sun Resort	Hotel 4-Star	
Garden Court Blackrock	Hotel 3-Star	(N)
Road Lodge Richards Bay	Hotel 2-Star	
The Oyster Box	Hotel 5-Star	
iSingizi Lodge	Lodge 3-Star	10 (N)
The Gorge Private Game Lodge & Spa	Lodge 4-Star	
Three Trees at Spioenkop	Lodge 4-Star	(N)
Hilton Durban	MESE* 5-Star	
aha Alpine Heath Resort	Self Catering Exclusive 4-Star	
Beverley Country Cottages	Self Catering Exclusive 3-Star	(N)
AM 171 Marula	Self Catering Exclusive 5-Star	(N)
Mpila Camp	Self Catering Shared 3-Star	

LIMPOPO

Name	CATEGORY	
Vhafamadi Bed and Breakfast	Bed & Breakfast 4-Star	
ATKV-Eiland Spa	Caravan & Camping 3-Star	
Mashutti Country Lodge	Country House 3-Star	(N)
Sherwood's Country House	Country House 4-Star	
Sondela Nature Reserve Guest House	Country House 5-Star	
AM Lodge - AM Villa - AM Spa	Game Lodge 5-Star	
Phelwana Game Lodge	Game Lodge 4-Star	11
Umlani Bushcamp	Game Lodge 3-Star	(N)
Cycad Guest House	Guest House 4-Star	
Fusion Boutique Hotel	Hotel 5-Star	
Protea Hotel Ranch Resort	Hotel 4-Star	
Timbavati Safari Lodge	Lodge 3-Star	
Town Lodge Polokwane	Hotel 3-Star	
Palala Boutique Game Lodge and Spa	Lodge 5-Star	
Zebula Golf Estate & Spa	Lodge 4-Star	
Swadini, A Forever Resort (Conference)	MESE* 3-Star	09
ATKV Klein-Kariba	Self Catering Exclusive 3-Star	
Zebula Golf Estate & Spa	Self Catering Exclusive 4-Star	(N)
ATKV-Eiland Spa	Self Catering Shared 3-Star	
Sondela Nature Reserve	Self Catering Shared 4-Star	

MPUMALANGA

Name	CATEGORY	
Visit Vakasha Guest Lodge 3	Backpacking & Hosteling 2-Star	
Hillwatering Country House	Bed & Breakfast 4-Star	
Matumi Golf Lodge	Bed & Breakfast 5-Star	
Visit Vakasha Guest Lodge 1	Bed & Breakfast 4-Star	(N)
Blyde Canyon, A Forever Resort	Caravan & Camping 3-Star	09
Welgelegen Manor	Country House 5-Star	
Bongani Mountain Lodge	Game Lodge 4-Star	
Jock Safari Lodge	Game Lodge 5-Star	(N)
Deletz Guest House	Guest House 5-Star	
Loerie's Call Guest House	Guest House 4-Star	
Turaco Lodge	Guest House 4-Star	
Casa Do Sol Hotel	Hotel 4-Star	
Protea Hotel Highveld	Hotel 3-Star	
Road Lodge Mbombela	Hotel 2-Star	
Needles Lodge	Lodge 4-Star	
Sabie River Bush Lodge	Lodge 3-Star	
115@Casambo	MESE* 5-Star	
Ingwenyama Conference & Sports Resort	MESE* 3-Star	(N)
Thaba Tsweni Lodge & Safaris	Self Catering Exclusive 3-Star	
The Cycad Lodge & Chalets	Self Catering Exclusive 4-Star	
Valbonne Villa at Tomjachu Bush Retreat	Self Catering Exclusive 3-Star	
Crystal Springs Mountain Lodge	Self Catering Shared 4-Star	

NORTH WEST

Name	CATEGORY	
Boubou Bed and Breakfast	Bed & Breakfast 4-Star	
ATKV Buffelspoort Holiday Resort	Caravan & Camping 4-Star	(N)
Bona Bona Game Lodge	Game Lodge 4-Star	
Etali Safari Lodge	Game Lodge 5-Star	
AnnVilla Guest House	Guest House 3-Star	
Franka Guesthouse	Guest House 4-Star	
Stirling Manor Boutique Guest House	Guest House 5-Star	
Road Lodge Potchefstroom	Hotel 2-Star	(N)
Orion Safari Lodge	Hotel 3-Star	
The Royal Marang Hotel	Hotel 5-Star	
Thaba Tshwene Game Lodge	Lodge 4-Star	
Anne's Place	Self Catering Exclusive 4-Star	
ATKV Buffelspoort Holiday Resort Chalets	Self Catering Exclusive 3-Star	

NORTHERN CAPE

Name	CATEGORY	
Brown's Manor	Bed & Breakfast 4-Star	(N)
Mattanu Private Game Reserve	Game Lodge 4-Star	
75 on Milner Lodge	Guest House 4-Star	
Kimberley Anne Small Luxury Hotel	Hotel 4-Star	
Oleander Guest House	Hotel 5-Star	08
Mittah Seperepere Convention Centre	MESE* 4-Star	
Naba Lodge Conference Facility	MESE* 3-Star	
Rhino Manor	Self Catering Exclusive 3-Star	

WESTERN CAPE

Name	CATEGORY	
Atlantic Point Backpackers	Backpacking & Hosteling 4-Star	
Green Elephant Backpackers	Backpacking & Hosteling 3-Star	
Saltycrax Backpackers	Backpacking & Hosteling 5-Star	(N)
Earthbound B&B	Bed & Breakfast 4-Star	
Knysna Herons Guest House	Bed & Breakfast 3-Star	
Plettenberg, A Forever Resort	Caravan & Camping 3-Star	09
De Doornkraal Historic Country House	Country House 4-Star	
Falcons View Manor	Country House 5-Star	(N)
Kunguru Lodge @ Tri Active	Lodge 3-Star	
Aquila Private Game Reserve	Game Lodge 4-Star	
Gondwana Lodge, Sanbona Wildlife Reserve	Game Lodge 5-Star	
African Oceans Manor on the Beach	Guest House 5-Star	
iKhaya Lodge & Conference Centre	Guest House 4-Star	
The THREE	Guest House 4-Star	
Franschhoek Boutique Hotel	Hotel 4-Star	
Protea Hotel Saldanha Bay	Hotel 3-Star	
Taj Cape Town	Hotel 5-Star	(N)
Town Lodge Bellville	Hotel 2-Star	
Tintswalo Atlantic Lodge	Lodge 5-Star	(N)
NH The Lord Charles Hotel	MESE* 4-Star	(N)
Makarios on Sea	Self Catering Exclusive 5-Star	
Orange Grove Farm	Self Catering Exclusive 5-Star	
Wolverfontein Cottages	Self Catering Exclusive 4-Star	
ATKV Goudini Spa - 4 star units	Self Catering Shared 4-Star	
Plettenberg, A Forever Resort (Chalets)	Self Catering Shared 3-Star	09

PRESENTING
ALL 2016 WINNERS

THE LILIZELA TOURISM AWARDS 2016

HONOURING
THE BEST OF THE BEST

VISITOR EXPERIENCE AWARDS

EASTERN CAPE	CATEGORY	
Bloukrans Bungy - Face Adrenalin	Action & Adventure	N
Chokka Trail	Beach Experience	N
Raggy Charters	Marine Adventure	N
Amapondo Backpackers	Roots & Culture	
Valley of Desolation	Scenic Beauty	
Sibuya Game Reserve-River Camp	Wildlife Encounters	📍

FREE STATE	CATEGORY
Pitseng Restaurant & Lounge	Culture & Lifestyle
Free State National Botanical Garden	Scenic Beauty
Cheetah Experience	Wildlife Encounters

GAUTENG	CATEGORY	
Johannesburg Skydiving Club	Action & Adventure	
SAB World of Beer	Culture & Lifestyle	
Lebo's Soweto	Roots & Culture	N
Walter Sisulu National Botanical Garden	Scenic Beauty	

KWAZULU-NATAL	CATEGORY	
Itchyfeet SA	Action & Adventure	📍
KwaZulu-Natal Sharks Board Maritime Centre	Marine Adventure	
Veyane Cultural Village and Accommodation	Roots & Culture	
Midlands Meander	Scenic Beauty	
Amakhosi Safari Lodge	Wildlife Encounters	

LIMPOPO	CATEGORY	
Shangri-la Country Hotel	Lap of Luxury	
Swadini, A Forever Resort	Scenic Beauty	📍 09

MPUMALANGA	CATEGORY	
Induna Adventures	Action & Adventure	
Emhlangeni Archery & Fishing	Culture & Lifestyle	
Matsamo Customs and Traditions Center	Roots & Culture	
Lowveld National Botanical Garden	Scenic Beauty	
Inyati Game Lodge	Wildlife Encounters	N

NORTH WEST	CATEGORY
Brauhaus am Damm	Culture & Lifestyle
Moruleng Cultural Precinct	Roots & Culture
Bill Harrop's "Original" Balloon Safaris	Action & Adventure
Etali Safari Lodge	Wildlife Encounters

NORTHERN CAPE	CATEGORY	
Gravity Adventures - Northern Cape	Action & Adventure	📍
The Big Hole	Roots & Culture	

WESTERN CAPE	CATEGORY	
AfriCanyon	Action & Adventure	
Boulders Beach Colony	Beach Experience	
Magic Moments in Oudtshoorn	Culture & Lifestyle	N
The Twelve Apostles Hotel and Spa	Lap of Luxury	N
Shark Diving Unlimited	Marine Adventure	
Richard's Supper Stage	Roots & Culture	
Cape Point, Table Mountain National Park	Scenic Beauty	N
Cango Wildlife Ranch	Wildlife Encounters	

TOUR OPERATOR AWARDS

AWARDEE	PROVINCE	CATEGORY		AWARDEE	PROVINCE	CATEGORY	
Imonti Tours	Eastern Cape	Tour Operator		Tim Brown Tours	KwaZulu-Natal	Tour Operator	
Ulysses Tours & Safaris cc	Gauteng	Tour Operator		Springbok Atlas Tours & Safaris	Western Cape	Tour Operator	N

TOURIST GUIDE AWARDS

AWARDEE	PROVINCE	CATEGORY		AWARDEE	PROVINCE	CATEGORY	
Velile Ndlumbini	Eastern Cape	Culture Guide		Raymond Khosa	Mpumalanga	Nature Guide	
Joseph Rantseke	Free State	Nature Guide		Thambe Mncedisi	North West	Culture Guide	
Nonkululeko Simelane	Gauteng	Culture Guide		Seleke Samuel	North West	Nature Guide	
Johannes Outram	KwaZulu-Natal	Adventure Guide		Kruger Marcus	North West	Adventure Guide	
Barry Fuller	KwaZulu-Natal	Culture Guide		Talita Kuhn	Northern Cape	Culture Guide	
Xolani Theophelus Gina	KwaZulu-Natal	Nature Guide		Kabelo Mothupi	Northern Cape	Nature Guide	
Sidney Fhumulani Mikosi	Limpopo	Nature Guide	N	James Fernie	Western Cape	Culture Guide	N
Bethuel Mkhonto	Mpumalanga	Nature Guide		Quinton Conroy	Western Cape	Nature Guide	

UNIVERSAL ACCESSIBILITY AWARDS

AWARDEE	PROVINCE	CATEGORY		AWARDEE	PROVINCE	CATEGORY	
Hluleka Nature Reserve	Eastern Cape	Accomm Mobility		Epic Enabled & Epic Guest House	Western Cape	Experience General	N
Soli Deo Gloria	Western Cape	Accomm Mobility	08 N	Access2africa Safaris	KwaZulu-Natal	Experience General	
Stormsriver Adv (Tsitsikamma Canopy Tour)	Eastern Cape	Experience General	📍	Flamingo Tours & Disabled Ventures	Western Cape	Experience Mobility	N

ETEYA AWARDS

AWARDEE	PROVINCE	CATEGORY		AWARDEE	PROVINCE	CATEGORY	
Drifters Raceway Theme Park	Eastern Cape	Culture Villages		Afrovibe Adventure Lodge	Western Cape	Accommodation	
Rochilla Guesthouse	Free State	Accommodation		Besty Travel	Limpopo	Nature Guides	08 N
Nnini Tours	Gauteng	Culture Villages		KwaBhekizihambi Guest House	Mpumalanga	Tour Operators	
La Teranga Bed And Breakfast	KwaZulu-Natal	Culture Villages					

B-BBEE AWARDS

AWARDEE	PROVINCE	CATEGORY	
Thaba Tshwene Game Lodge	North West	Exempted Micro Enterprise (EME) Under R5 Million	N
Lucette Boutique Guest House	Free State	Exempted Micro Enterprise (EME) Under R5 Million	
Stormsriver Adventures (Tsitsikamma Canopy Tour)	Eastern Cape	Qualifying Small Enterprise (QSE) R5 – R45 Million	📍 N
Villa Maria Guest Lodge	North West	Qualifying Small Enterprise (QSE) R5 – R45 Million	
Cape Town International Convention Centre Company	Western Cape	Large Enterprise Over R45 Million	N

Note: National Award winners are highlighted. N 08 **See page numbers for more info.**

Voted
SOUTH AFRICA'S BEST

THE
LILIZELA
TOURISM AWARDS
2016

IT'S THE **CHERRY** ON TOP

WE LOVE MAKING PEOPLE SMILE.
WHEN THIS PASSION TRANSLATES
INTO AWARDS, IT MAKES US SMILE.

Forever once again received multiple
nominations and accolades at the recent
Lilizela Tourism Awards, and it's all
thanks to your on-going loyalty and support.

OUR NATIONAL LILIZELA AWARD WINNERS ARE:

GARIEP – **Winner** of the Best 3 star Self-catering Shared Vacation in SA category

PLETTENBERG – **Winner** of the Best 3 star Caravan and Camping in SA category

OUR PROVINCIAL LILIZELA AWARD WINNERS ARE:

SWADINI – Awarded Service Excellence Awards for Scenic Beauty and 3 star MESE in Limpopo

BLYDE CANYON – Awarded Service Excellence Award for 3 star Caravan and Camping in Mpumalanga

GARIEP – Awarded Service Excellence Awards for 3 star Caravan and Camping, 3 star Self-catering Shared Vacation and 3 star MESE in the Free State

PLETTENBERG – Awarded Service Excellence Awards for 3 star Caravan and Camping and 3 star Self-catering Shared Vacation in the Western Cape

AND OUR PROVINCIAL FINALISTS ARE:

- Badplaas – FINALIST – 3 star Caravan & Camping | Hotel MESE | Self-catering Shared Vacation
- Blyde Canyon – FINALIST – 3 star Caravan & Camping | MESE Self-catering Shared Vacation
- Forever Hotel @ Centurion – FINALIST – 4 star Hotel | MESE
- Loskopdam – FINALIST – 3 star Caravan & Camping | MESE
- Matombu Wild – FINALIST – 5 star Self-catering Exclusive
- Mount Sheba – FINALIST – 3 star Lodge
- Tshipise – FINALIST – 3 star Caravan & Camping | Self-catering Shared Vacation
- Warmbaths – FINALIST – 3 star Caravan & Camping | Self-catering Shared Vacation
- Waterfall Safari Lodge – FINALIST – 3 star Lodge

CELEBRATING
OUR
WINNERS

THANK YOU
FOR VOTING FOR US

FOREVER
RESORTS · LODGES · HOTELS · RETREATS

Tel: +27(0)12 423 5600
Email: info@foreversa.co.za
www.foreversa.co.za

Voted

SOUTH AFRICA'S BEST

THE LILIZELA TOURISM AWARDS 2016

PHELWANA GAME LODGE

The year 2013 marked the 75th anniversary of the De Villiers family having been part of South Africa's lowveld history, and today we are proud to have been recognised as a Provincial Award winner and national finalist in the 2016 Lilizela Tourism Awards for being one of the best 4-star game lodges in the country.

Phelwana Game Lodge is perfectly situated in the Hoedspruit area of the Limpopo Province. Located a mere 40 kilometres from the Kruger National Parks Orpen Gate, The Blyde River Canyon and the nearby Timbavati Private Nature Reserve, Phelwana is the perfect destination for guests wanting to relax in the South African Bushveld.

At our 46 Sleeper Luxury Game Lodge, we offer our guests a variety of accommodation offerings, ranging from tented camp to bush villa accommodation, all with private swimming pools. Guests can enjoy a variety of activities such as bird watching, game drives, bush walks, cycling and fishing in this leisurely environment or arrange day trips to the surrounding area to see what South Africa has to offer.

By embracing the ethos of conservation and well known for our hospitality and attention to detail, the De Villiers family offer you Phelwana Game Lodge. Your place in the Bushveld!

For bookings call +27 (0)15 793 2475 or email book@phelwana.co.za or for more information visit www.phelwana.co.za.

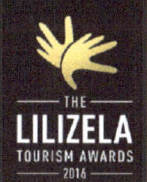

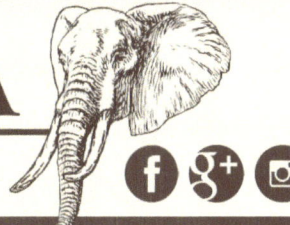

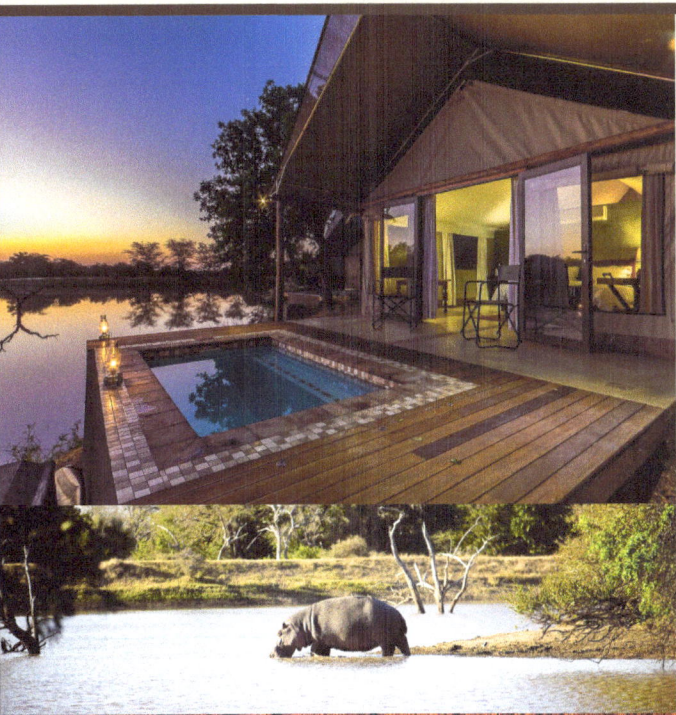

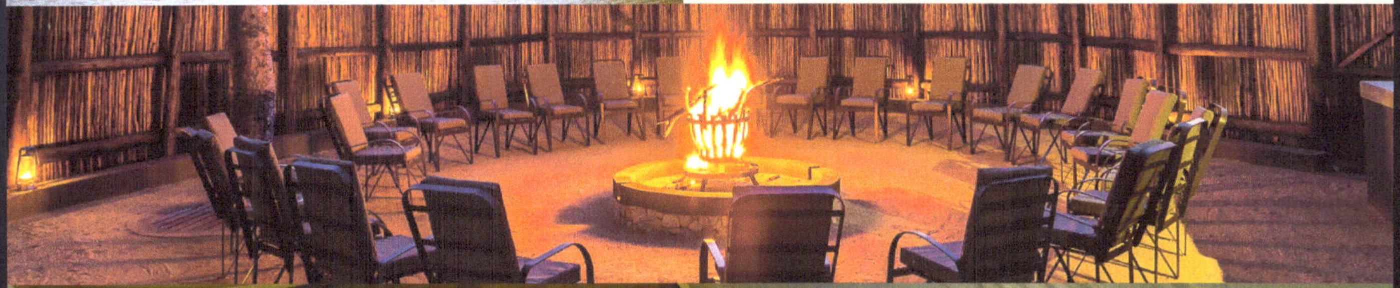

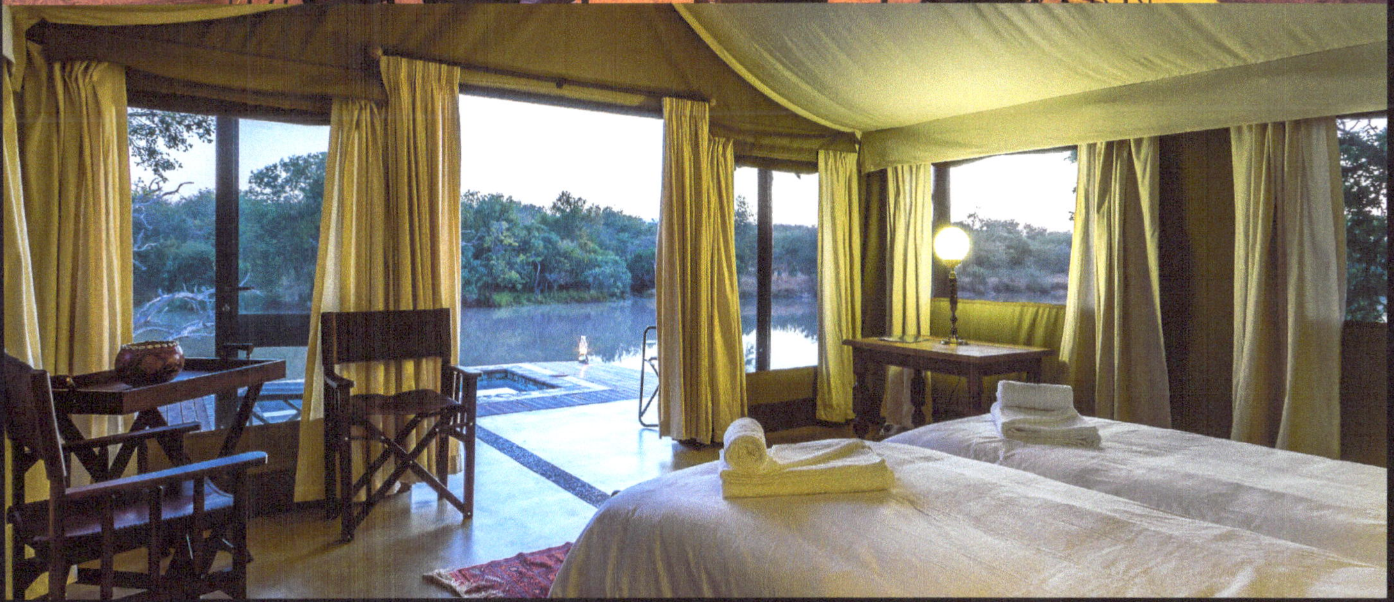

Rhulani Safari Lodge - South Africa

Banyan Tree Ras Al Khaimah Beach Hotel - United Arab Emirates

Conrad Maldives Rangali Island - Maldive

White Pearl Resorts - Mozambique

Head over Hills Luxury Retreat - South A

A Decade Of Awarding
SERVICE
EXCELLENCE

Celebrating its 10th anniversary this year, the 2016 **World Luxury Hotel Awards** took place at the exquisite St. Regis Doha in Qatar on 29 October, where some of the world's leading hotels gathered to be recognised on stage for their outstanding efforts.

Awards are presented to luxury hotels in over 60 categories on a country, regional, continent and global basis. The objectives of these awards are to recognise and celebrate service excellence, to encourage key players to strive to new heights and to grow global competitiveness in the industry.

Considered the pinnacle of achievement for hoteliering, the World Luxury Hotel Awards sets the basis for service standards around the globe and prides itself on providing true recognition to luxury hotels and resorts in their relevant categories. Furthermore, the public is given a voice that counts, as international tour operators, travel agents and hotel guests are afforded the opportunity to vote annually for their favourite destinations and elect the final winners. Voting is based on facilities and service excellence and hotels are encouraged to conduct voting campaigns in order to garner guest votes.

"There is no greater reward for a hotel and its' staff than being bestowed with a World Luxury Hotel Award, as voted for by their own guests. It is the most gratifying review in its truest form." says Anton Perold, Managing Director.

And it's not hard to see why these luxury hotels are nominated to compete, they offer everything and more that the discerning traveller is looking for. Feel like you need some time away? Why not book at a World Luxury Hotel Award winning property.

To view more award winning hotels or for more information on participating in these prestigious awards, please visit *www.luxuryhotelawards.com*

PARTNER FEATURE

VEHICLE RENTAL MOTY AWARDS
WINNERS

Robert Wright - Regional After Sales Manager for the Volkswagen Brand; Carla Wentzel - General Manager: Sales and Marketing for the Volkswagen Brand; Loshini Pillay - Manager: National Key Accounts for the Volkswagen Brand and Stanley Netshituka - Manager: National Special Markets for the Volkswagen Brand with SAVRALA awards.

The South African Vehicle Rental and Leasing Association (SAVRALA) has announced Volkswagen as the Manufacturer of The Year (MOTY) in the car rental sector for the seventh consecutive year. The revered SAVRALA's MOTY award recognises exceptional levels of service, new standards in technology and safety as well as continuous improvements in service delivery by vehicle manufacturers.

Volkswagen was presented with the award at the 21st edition of the annual SAVRALA gala dinner which was held in Johannesburg on October 21.

Volkswagen was the biggest winner on the night as it also walked away with other key awards which included the Value Award, Best Account Executive for Loshini Pillay and Best Manufacturer's Technical Representative for Robert Wright.

Audi won the Tutuka award for the second year in a row. The award is presented to a premium brand that has demonstrated commitment to satisfying the needs of customers in the niche and lower volume segment.

The recipients of the SAVRALA awards are decided through a stringent process by rental companies such as Avis Budget, Bidvest,

Hertz, Europcar /Tempest, Thrifty and First Car. These companies are required to rate 26 motor manufacturers that they interact with using a survey containing different and targeted questions ranging from aspects such as communication, contact with the manufacturer, technical assistance, parts availability and pricing structures.

The President of SAVRALA, Marc Corcoran lauded Volkswagen for its remarkable achievement. Corcoran said: "It is a remarkable achievement and testimony to the Volkswagen team that they have continued to defend its MOTY leadership for a seventh time. They are true brand custodians and should take great pride at the fact that the car rental industry has recognised and duly rewarded their efforts."

Thomas Schaefer, Chairman and Managing Director of Volkswagen Group South Africa said: "Volkswagen is honoured and humbled to be recognised by the car rental companies for the seventh consecutive year. Members of SAVRALA are one of our key customers and we are very grateful for their recognition with the MOTY award as well as their continued support of our products." t

For more information visit www.savrala.co.za

#SAMOTY16
AWARD SUMMARY

Overall Bronze
Toyota South Africa Motors

Overall Silver
Hyundai South Africa

Overall Gold
Volkswagen South Africa

Best Account Executive
Loshini Pillay (Volkswagen)

Best Manufacturer's Technical Representative
Robert Wright (Volkswagen)

Most Improved
Hyundai

Value Award (Certificate)
Volkswagen

Tutuka Award
Audi South Africa

PARTNER FEATURE

SPORTS & EVENTS TOURISM AWARDS
WINNERS

Best Internat
that contr
tourism

Winner of the Best International Event That Contributes to Tourism Growth: Cape Town Cycle Tour.

The evening of the 26th October 2016 saw the inaugural Sports & Events Tourism Awards take place in the City of Tshwane – an initiative launched alongside the annual SETE 2016 conference.

By **Paul W. Reynell.**

Entries were submitted by host cities, event owners and sponsors and submissions included impact assessment reports.

An evaluation panel made up of event tourism experts and national government institutions adjudicated each submission and a shortlist of the nominees were invited to the Awards Dinner.

The winners in the various categories are:

1. **Best Emerging Township Event Contributing to Local Economic Development**

   WINNER: **Kasi Career Expo**

2. **Best Event Leaving a Development Legacy**

   WINNER: **Dance Umbrella – Dance Forum**

   RUNNER UP: **Momentum Ekasi Challenge**

3. **Best Domestic Event Contributing to Tourism Growth**

   WINNER: **Arnold Classic Africa**

   RUNNER UP: **Karoo Food Festival**

4. **Best Event Improving the Brand Profile of the Destination**

   WINNER: **Red Bull X-Fighters**

5. **Best International Event that Contributes to Tourism Growth**

   WINNER: **Cape Town Cycle Tour**

For more information visit www.sportsandevents.co.za

About the Author: Paul W. Reynell is a Client Service Director at Paddington Station PR who handle public relations for the Sports & Events Tourism Exchange conference on behalf of Thebe Reed Exhibitions.

Winner of the Best Event Leaving a Development Legacy: Dance Umbrella.

Market Intelligence Report

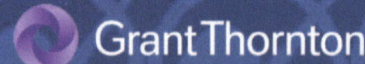

The information below was extracted from data available as at **20 October 2016**. By **Martin Jansen van Vuuren** of **Grant Thornton**.

ARRIVALS

The latest available data from **Statistics South Africa** is for **January to August 2016***:

	Current period	Change over same period last year
UK	285 230	11.5%
Germany	174 163	20.7%
USA	229 327	18.6%
India	66 175	27.0%
China (incl Hong Kong)	78 837	64.2%
Overseas Arrivals	1 574 470	19.7%
African Arrivals	5 043 294	13.4%
Total Foreign Arrivals	6 625 141	14.8%

HOTEL STATS

The latest available data from **STR Global** is for **January** to **August 2016**:

Current period	Average Room Occupancy (ARO)	Average Room Rate (ARR)	Revenue Per Available Room (RevPAR)
All Hotels in SA	63.0%	R 1 157	R 729
All 5-star hotels in SA	64.5%	R 2 124	R 1 370
All 4-star hotels in SA	62.2%	R 1 068	R 664
All 3-star hotels in SA	63.1%	R 916	R 578
Change over same period last year			
All Hotels in SA	3.2%	9.1%	12.7%
All 5-star hotels in SA	5.6%	11.0%	17.2%
All 4-star hotels in SA	4.3%	6.6%	11.1%
All 3-star hotels in SA	3.0%	6.3%	9.6%

ACSA DATA

The latest available data from **ACSA** is for **August 2016**:

Change over same period last year	Passengers arriving on International Flights	Passengers arriving on Regional Flights	Passengers arriving on Domestic Flights
OR Tambo International	3.0%	4.5%	6.1%
Cape Town International	11.1%	24.6%	6.6%
King Shaka International	19.3%	N/A	9.3%

CAR RENTAL DATA

The latest available data from **SAVRALA** is for **January to June 2015**:

	Current period	Change over same period last year
Industry rental days	8 139 127	-1%
Industry utilisation	70.2%	-0.7%
Industry Average daily revenue	2 498 944 728	1%

WHAT THIS MEANS FOR MY BUSINESS

For the first time the data from Stats SA, STR and ACSA all reflect the same period. The data indicates the recovery of international arrivals from 2015 as reflected in the growth in Stats SA data, growth in the rates of 5-star hotels and growth in the arrivals on international and regional flights. The domestic tourism market has also grown as reflected in the growth in the rates of 3-star hotels and arrivals on domestic flights.

*Note that African Arrivals plus Overseas Arrivals do not add to Total Foreign Arrivals due to the exclusion of unspecified arrivals, which could not be allocated to either African or Overseas.

For more information contact Martin at Grant Thornton on +27 (0)21 417 8838 or visit: http://www.gt.co.za

TOURISM
BUSINESS INDEX

Mainstreaming Travel and Tourism in the South African Economy

Image courtesy of South African Tourism

The Tourism Business Index for the third quarter of 2016 shows improved business performance, buoyed by a positive showing in South Africa's accommodation sector.

By **Kagiso Mosue.**

The Tourism Business Council of South Africa (TBCSA) represents businesses operating in South Africa's travel and tourism industry, whose total contribution to the country's GDP stood at 9.4% in 2015 or R375 billion. In the same period, the industry's total contribution to employment, including jobs directly supported by the industry was 9.9% of total employment or 1,554,000 jobs – this is expected to rise to 1,557,000 jobs this year.

The latest report for the third quarter (Q3) of 2016 shows a slight uptick in the industry's overall business performance, buoyed by positive results in the accommodation sector. However, the index score is still somewhat below 'normal' levels of acceptable performance.

'Normal' is calibrated to an index of 100 and results higher than 100 are an indication of better than normal performance (and vice versa). In Q3 the industry recorded an overall index score of 92.6 - achieving an index score which is below normal performance levels but was better than the forecast score of 84.7. The index score achieved in this quarter is also an improvement from an index score of 78.9 that was achieved in Q2 2016.

TBI comprises two sub-indices namely: accommodation and 'other tourism businesses' and the positive results achieved in this quarter are largely thanks to the positive performance score of 109 recorded by the accommodation sub-index,

against the anticipated score of 105. The 'other tourism businesses' sub-index (all other tourism businesses excluding accommodation) recorded lower than normal business performance, recording an index score of 80 in this quarter.

Commenting on the performance of the accommodation sector, Chairman of the National Accommodation Association of SA (NAA-SA) Donovan Muirhead, says the feedback he's received from members is that "the months of July and August were great periods, however September was a bit more challenging with occupancies and revenue per available room averaging a similar figure to last year."

Federated Hospitality Association of Southern Africa (FEDHASA) CEO, Tshifhiwa Tshivengwa added that results of the accommodation sub-index needed to be contextualised. "If there is an increase in bed nights, this could be attributed to corporate and inbound travellers. However, the fact that we are experiencing normal or acceptable business performance does not mean we are where we need to be. The cost of labour is still high; the cost of electricity is higher than inflation. If we deduct these two (factors), we might see that we are not doing so well."

Contributing Factors

Whilst the issue of immigration regulations is topical right now, the index report highlights other factors which contributed negatively to performance in Q3, confirming

Tshivengwa's concerns. They are the cost of inputs (a recurring issue); the cost of labour and issues related to competitive market behaviour.

Elaborating on the challenges in the operating environment, Gillian Saunders, Head of Advisory Services at Grant Thornton says "local economic growth is seriously constrained and this impacts directly on business travel which is the mainstay of many businesses in the tourism sector. This, coupled with government reigning in the travel and conferencing costs means many businesses are seeing lower domestic demand levels and rate pressure".

But, it is not all doom and gloom as respondents of the 'other tourism businesses' sub-index highlight: 61% attribute the weak Rand exchange rate as a positive contributing factor; followed by 50% who cited strong overseas leisure demand and 29% who mentioned strong overseas business demand as a positive contributing factors.

Outlook for Q4

Looking ahead into the last quarter, expectations remain somewhat subdued, judging by the overall TBI prediction of 87.1. The accommodation and car hire sectors are expected to continue their good form, achieving index scores of 109.4 and 134.1 respectively. In contrast, the overall index score for 'other tourism businesses' is expected to continue the decline with a forecasted index of 69.9.

About the Author: Kagiso Mosue is the Corporate Communications Manager for the Tourism Business Council of South Africa.
www.tbcsa.travel

Global Destinations Welcome Nearly
One Billion Tourists

Destinations around the world welcomed 956 million international tourists between January and September 2016. According to the latest UNWTO World Tourism Barometer, this is 34 million (4%) more than the same 2015 period.

Demand for international tourism remained robust in the first nine months of 2016, though growing at a somewhat more moderate pace. After a strong start of the year, growth was slower in the second quarter of 2016 to pick up again in the third quarter of the year. While most destinations report encouraging results, others continue to struggle with the impact of negative events, either in their country or in their region.

Regional results

Asia and the Pacific led growth across world regions, with international tourist arrivals (overnight visitors) up 9% through September. All four subregions shared in this growth. Many destinations reported double-digit growth, with the Republic of Korea (+34%), Vietnam (+36%), Japan (+24%) and Sri Lanka (+15%) in the lead.

In Europe, international arrivals grew by 2% between January and September 2016, with solid growth in most destinations. Nonetheless, double-digit increases in major destinations such as Spain, Hungary, Portugal and Ireland were offset by feeble results in France, Belgium and Turkey. As a consequence, Northern Europe grew by 6% and Central and Eastern Europe by 5% while results were weaker in Western Europe (-1%) and Southern Mediterranean Europe (+0%).

By **Rut Gomez Sobrino**.

International tourist arrivals in the Americas increased by 4% through September. South America (+7%) and Central America (+6%) led results, followed closely by the Caribbean and North America (both +4%).

In Africa (+8%), sub-Saharan destinations rebounded strongly throughout the year, while North Africa picked up in the third quarter. Available data for the Middle East points to a 6% decrease in arrivals, though results vary from destination to destination. Results started to gradually improve in the second half of the year in both North Africa and the Middle East.

Strong demand for outbound travel

The great majority of leading source markets in the world reported increases in international tourism expenditure during the first three to nine months of 2016.

Among the top five source markets, China, the world's top source market, continues to drive demand, reporting double-digit growth in spending (+19%). Likewise, robust results come from the United States (+9%), which benefited many destinations in the Americas and beyond. Germany reported a 5% increase in expenditure, the United Kingdom, a 10% increase, and France, 3% growth.

In the remainder of the top ten, tourism spending grew notably in Australia and the

Republic of Korea (both +9%), and moderately in Italy (+3%). By contrast, expenditure from the Russian Federation declined 37% and from Canada a slight 2%.

Beyond the top 10, eight other markets reported double-digit growth: Egypt (+38%), Argentina (+27%), Spain (+19%), India (+16%), Thailand (+15%), Ukraine (+15%), Ireland (+12%) and Norway (+11%).

Prospects remain positive

Prospects remain positive for the remaining quarter of 2016 according to the UNWTO Confidence Index.

The members of the UNWTO Panel of Tourism Experts are confident about the September-December period, mostly in Africa, the Americas and Asia and the Pacific. Experts in Europe and the Middle East are somewhat more cautious. **t**

Note: Results reflect preliminary data reported to date and are subject to revision.

About the Author: Rut Gomez Sobrino *is a Media Officer at the World Tourism Organization (UNWTO), a United Nations specialized agency, and the leading international organization with a decisive and central role in promoting the development of responsible, sustainable and universally accessible tourism. It serves as a global forum for tourism policy issues and is a practical source of tourism know-how. Its membership includes 157 countries, 6 territories, 2 permanent observers and over 500 Affiliate Members. www.unwto.org*

The winning 'Like' or 'Share' during the month of **November 2016** will receive **2 Kenyan Scarfs** with the compliments of **Livingstones Supply Co** – *Suppliers of the Finest Products to the Hospitality Industry*.

'Like' / 'Share' / 'Connect' with these Social Media icons to win!

Livingston Supply Company

TourismTattler

Competition Rules: Only one winner will be selected each month on a random selection draw basis. The prize winner will be notified via social media. The prize will be delivered by the sponsor to the winners postal address within South Africa. Should the winner reside outside of South Africa, delivery charges may be applicable. The prize may not be exchanged for cash.

Win

Beautiful scarf made from 100% Viscose, 35 x 160cm. Produced locally from imported fabric in a range of exquisitely woven patterns. The vibrant and rich as well soft and muted colours reflecting the beauty and ethnicity of the African nature and culture. These may be worn to temper the evening or morning chill or to keep cool in the African sun. Adding elegance, style, comfort and functionality to any wardrobe.

Congratulations to our October 2016 Social Media winner

Winner

@PlettGameRes

Plett Game Reserve offers Big-5 Game Drives, Horse Safaries, and Accommodation in Plettenberg Bay, Garden Route, South Africa. **Plett Game Reserve** will receive **2 CDs**: **1x Essential South African Jazz** (the Jo'burg sessions) **CD** *plus* **1x Songs & Stories of Africa CD** with the compliments of **Livingstones Supply Co** – *Suppliers of the Finest Products to the Hospitality Industry.*

For more information visit *www.livingstonessupplyco.co.za*

New Blood Lions & Wild Dogs at
SA World Heritage Site

By **Debbie Cooper.**

A coalition of three male lions was collared and released from their holding boma into the uMkhuze section of the South Africa's first world heritage site, the iSimangaliso Wetland Park, late on the 18th of October 2016.

Big Cats

The lions, from the Tswalu Kalahari Reserve are genetically distinct from the pride of 16 lions presently residing in iSimangaliso, all of which are from the same blood line. The lions remained in the boma for several weeks before being released to acquaint themselves with the existing pride.

This introduction boosts the establishment of a viable population in iSimangaliso after the last lion was shot by conservationists some 47 years ago for going "rogue" in what was then an unfenced park. The first lion introductions back to iSimangaliso took place in December 2013 and 2014 respectively.

The first family of four lions - translocated from Tembe Elephant Park - were released in December 2013 and comprised an adult female and three sub-adult offspring. Their arrival catapulted iSimangaliso to 'Big 7' status. This was followed by the coalition of two males (brothers) and three females during the course of 2014.

In order to slow down the breeding rate of the lions, the females underwent partial hysterectomies which is the removal of one horn of the uterus. Lions breed prolifically and this action should halve the number of litters obviating the need for translocations to other parks in the short-term. Since December 2013, three sets of cubs have swelled the ranks.

iSimangaliso now generates some 7% of the province's tourism GDP and over 7 000 direct permanent tourism jobs.

All iSimangaliso's adult lions are fitted with satellite collars to monitor their movements for biological and safety reasons. They are tracked daily by Park staff supported by Wildlife Act volunteers with the information feeding into Park management.

Wild Dogs

One of the most exciting sightings in the uMkhuze section of iSimangaliso Wetland Park is that of the endangered wild dog (or African Painted Dog). With an estimated 1400 fully grown adult dogs left globally, the two packs that have been established in iSimangaliso's uMkhuze form a vital part of South Africa's metapopulation. A new litter of 14 healthy pups has been spotted and photographed in the last few days.

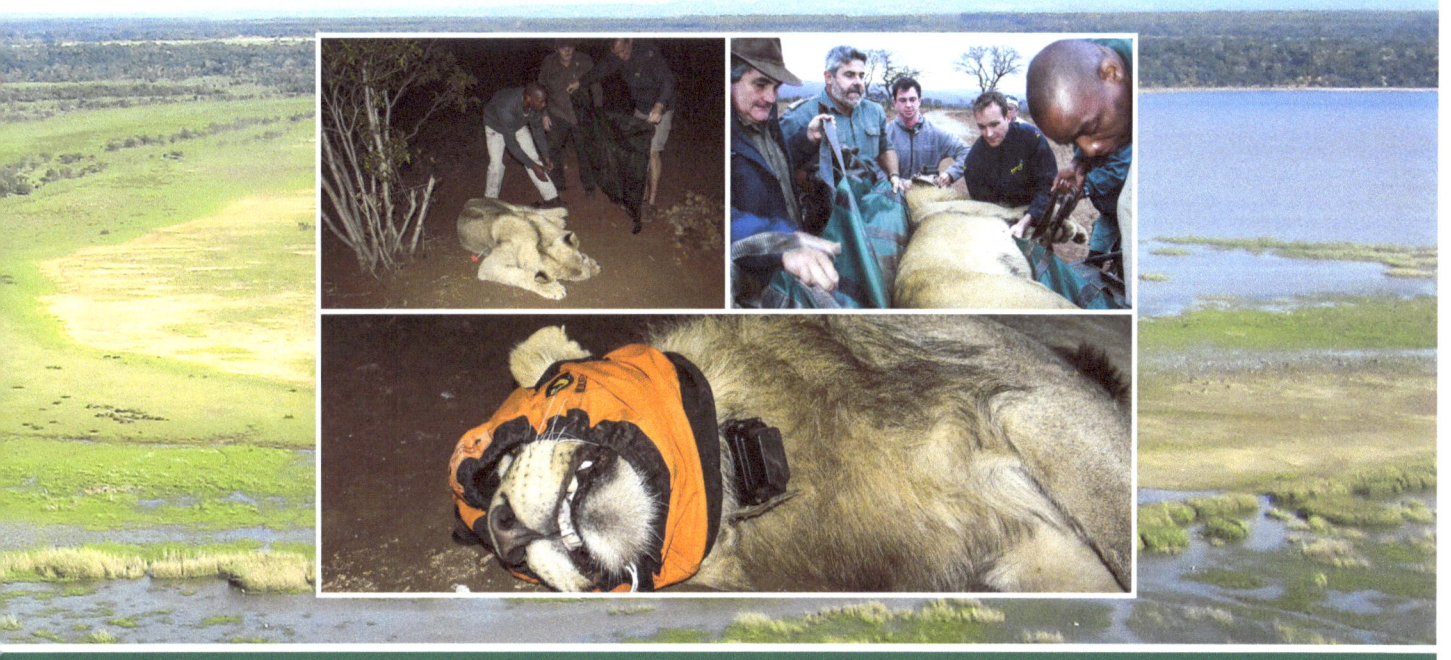

Cheetah Success Story

Another special resident of uMkhuze is the cheetah, a reintroduction success story despite initial challenges. Cheetah are categorised as vulnerable by the IUCN with a population of around 1500 adults in South Africa. Today, fifteen individuals live within this area some of which have tracking collars to assist management. There is a good chance of seeing these on a game drive within the park, especially while the vegetation is still so sparse. On Wednesday 19 October, no fewer than four individuals were spotted, while the previous weekend a visitor at the Mantuma Rest Camp captured photographs of a magnificent cheetah within metres of the huts.

Additional Facts

Several thousand heads of game have been translocated by iSimangaliso into the Park with the support of Ezemvelo KZN Wildlife since 2000. All the game that historically occurred in the region (including oribi, tsessebe, black and white rhino, elephant, wild dog, cheetah, buffalo, waterbuck and blue wildebeest) with the exception of eland, have now been re-introduced.

Much of this work has been undertaken by community SMMEs, creating significant employment in an area marked by unemployment and poverty. Fencing was done by agreement with communities, involving negotiations with seven traditional council chiefs and dozens of isigodi's (wards).

For over a century, the uMkhuze section of iSimangaliso has protected wildlife and biodiversity. Through flood and drought, political upheaval and disease, this remarkable 37 000 ha portion of the World Heritage Site has endured and displayed the utmost resilience. The soils are some of the richest to be found, regularly recovering from the stark barren destitution of drought periods to an abundance of nutritious grasses in times of rainfall. uMkhuze was renowned as one of the two last remaining bastions of black rhino in the 1960's before the campaign to repopulate other areas.

Currently emerging from the worst recorded drought of our times, there is no doubt that uMkhuze will complete the natural cycle of rejuvenation, with the gradual return of spring rains bringing about a natural transformation. The rewilding process is almost complete and with all tourist network roads completely re-tarred and gravelled, the rebuild of hides, ablutions, the Fig Forest Walk and other visitor attractions and a new eMshophi Gate building well underway, this section of the Park is proudly placed as one of iSimangaliso's greatest jewels. t

About the author: **Debbie Cooper** *is the Executive Assistant to the CEO of iSimangaliso. Debbie's roots are in conservation and travel writing and she has been an integral part of the iSimangaliso team for eleven years. She's a writer and keen photographer, committed to the conservation of South Africa's first World Heritage Site.*

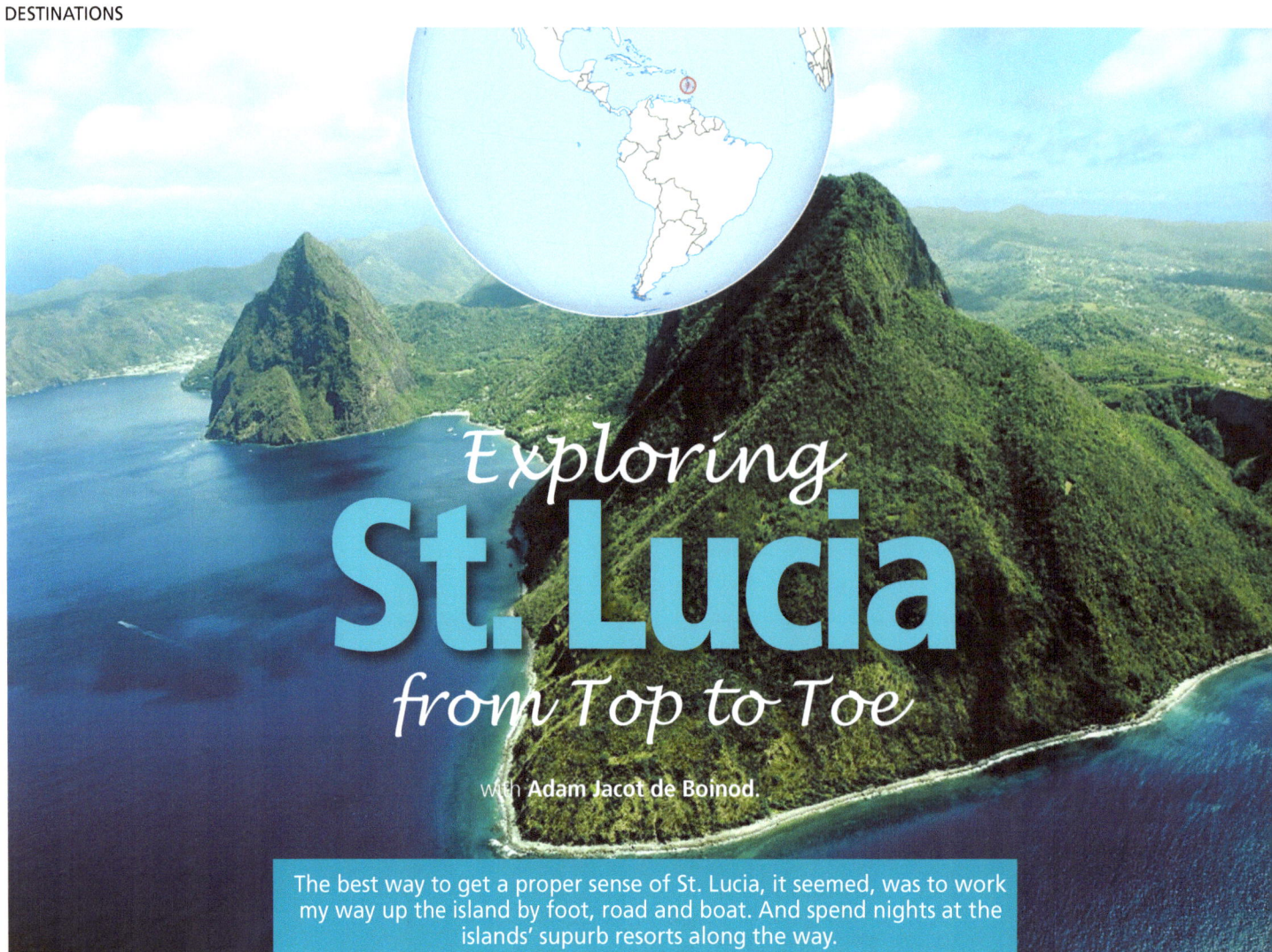

Exploring
St. Lucia
from Top to Toe

with **Adam Jacot de Boinod.**

The best way to get a proper sense of St. Lucia, it seemed, was to work my way up the island by foot, road and boat. And spend nights at the islands' supurb resorts along the way.

More than anywhere St. Lucia is best visited by being on the move. The thing to do is to change hotels every few days. For all its beauty and fecundity, the island can be quite restrictive especially if you want to stretch a leg as the beaches are small and the hillsides are steep. Each cove (which the French called *anse*) is a hideaway and hotels vie to offer the most romantic setting.

Attempting to traverse the island on foot, I descended steeply down from hills still stricken with their trees deracinated from a recent storm.

Viceroy Sugar Beach Resort

Starting from the international airport in the south I reached the Viceroy Sugar Beach. This American hotel has surely secured the choice location of the island. It's between the famous twin peaks of Gros and Petit Piton. These upright, precipitous mountains reach over two thousand feet in height and are the consequence of an historic earthquake balancing its neighbouring sea with equal depth. They gave me a sense of being grounded with their majestic presence dwarfing all below. I needed to see them

panoramically. From the sea as well as the land. At different angles they alternate between one being a pyramid and the other a multi-faceted shape.

At the Gardens I came across a beaten track to a 50 foot waterfall with the water free falling every second for eternity. I learnt even more about nature from the 250 year old 'Sulphur Springs' still bubbling away, emitting noxious fumes that gave it's name to *Soufrière*. This island's second town is further north and is small and jolly with shops behind her seafront and houses receding up into the valley.

Capella Marigot Bay

The Capella Marigot Bay hotel's location couldn't be more idyllic as it overlooks its marina. Here I got a strong sense of the nautical character of St. Lucia as I looked around at premier yachts berthed from all over the world. The bay is known as *'hurricane hole'* from its position on the west side of the island. It's surrounded by mountains and experiences minimal tidal changes. Yachties tinker with their equipment and there's a serenity in this secluded and secure haven. A serenity reflected in the philosophy of the hotel.

As I moved up the island the vegetation changes and the sand gets whiter.

St. James's Morgan Bay

Next came St. James's Morgan Bay. The rooms have double balconies and it is beautifully set within the sound of lapping waves and has views of the sea offering stunning sunsets. It's for those preferring organised entertainment. There's a spoiling range of six restaurants and

Image: Capella Marigot Bay Resort

always somewhere open to eat. Le Jardin is for the fine diners while the Bamboo has fabulous seafood salads. They lent me a sailing catamaran and off I went after one lesson. How liberating! And with their rescue service how reassuring!

Cap Maison

Next I worked my way past Castries the capital and on to Cap Maison. This classy boutique villa resort has a Mediterranean feel, where Spanish meets Moroccan. Walking beneath crenellated roofs, past trickling fountains, under vaulted brick corridors and through inner courtyards with birds twittering, I half expected to be responding to peeling church bells. Once a private house it has been cleverly extended. It is located on the northernmost tip in Cap Estate, a highly exclusive area.

There's dramatic cliff scenery with the tranquil waters of the Caribbean Sea on one side and the brisk Atlantic Ocean to the other. The grounds are tropically landscaped with carpet-mossy grass. Chef Nico for the Cliff at Cap restaurant offers a delicious seafood chowder. Champagne is delivered in a basket to diners fifty feet below via a zipwire. Very James Bond! And with zipwire excursions all across the island – very St, Lucia.

Pigeon Island

I took a trip to Pigeon Island. It is like a miniature version of the Pitons with her two humped hills. It was joined up to the mainland in the 1960s by a causeway that is now a picturesque tree-lined avenue. Pigeon Island thankfully wasn't turned into an hotel but has been preserved for the common good. While Lord Glenconner of Mustique

fame sold the land between the Pitons to a hotel, no money would allow another scenic part of the island to pass hands. This is a northern cove, nicknamed 'Five Dollar Beach', which is what the 90 year-old owner charges each visitor to enjoy his unspoilt coastline with its biggest of fish and whitest of sand. No number of multiple dollar offers has managed to take it off his hands.

I returned back down the Atlantic coast to the accompaniment of the brightest rainbow I had ever witnessed. A magnificent send off to such a colourful island. The calm after the storm! 🅣

About the author: Tourism Tattler correspondent, **Adam Jacot de Boinod** worked for Stephen Fry on the first series of QI, the BBC programme. Adam is the author of The Meaning of Tingo and Other Extraordinary Words from around the World, published by Penguin Books. While researching this article, Adam travelled via Gatwick Express (www.gatwickexpress.com) with support from The Holiday Place (www.holidayplace.co.uk) and the St Lucia Tourist Board (www.saintluciauk.org)

Child Friendly Safaris

Many parents dream of taking their children on a once-in a-lifetime safari adventure holiday, but most South African Big-5 game reserves and lodges have a minimum age restriction rule for children. Fortunately there are exceptions to this and Lalibela Private Game Reserve in the malaria-free province of the Eastern Cape is one such exception.

By **Vernon Wait.**

Mark's Camp at Lalibela welcomes families and was specifically constructed for families with young children under the age of 12 years. The other two lodges on the reserve, namely Lentaba Lodge and Tree Tops (with a fourth lodge currently under construction) have been kept for guests who would prefer not to have the sound of young voices disturb the peace of the bush.

Child-friendly Game Drives

Children aged 8 years and over are welcome to join the adults on the adult game drive. Children aged between 2 and 7 years enjoy their own game drives and that's where the fun begins for these Generation-Z* 'Rainbow Children' – after all, what 2-year-old wants to sit still and keep quite while adults zoom their cameras at a slumbering pride of lion? The children's game drive has been specially designed for young children, with their own game ranger, Children's Programme Coordinator, and game-viewing vehicle. The game drives are shorter than those of the adults. Due to the unpredictability of small children, care is also taken to avoid getting close to dangerous animals. Children may still see the Big-5 from a distance but the primary focus of the children's game drive is on plains game (antelope, giraffe and zebra), bird and insect species. It is a sensory safari and exposes the children to the sights, smells, sounds, feel and taste of Africa.

Child-friendly Activities

In between meals and game drives, children over 2 years of age are kept busy with a number of fun and educational activities, such as rhino T-shirt painting, making African masks, painting, making photo frames, making wind mobiles, and a lot more. While the children's programme is run separately to that of the adults, parents and older siblings can join in on the children's activities, although the parents would most likely want to enjoy the peace and tranquillity of the lodge and sunbathe on loungers beside one of the two swimming pools while their children are being entertained. Experienced child minders and nannies are available to take care of children under 2 while adults are on game drive, as toddlers aren't allowed on any of the game drives.

Child-friendly Family Accommodation

Mark's Camp has several stone and thatch family chalets (ideally suited to families with children aged 2 to 11 years), which have a large bedroom with two single children's beds separated from the parents' luxury king-size bed by a partition, a bathroom with bath and shower, and separate toilet. There is also a family suite, which has 2 en-suite bedrooms and a lounge with 2 day beds. All family chalets and the family suite have private outdoor decks with secure balustrades overlooking the verdant bush and birdlife, and are equipped with tea/coffee stations, and a desk and chair. Complimentary guest bathroom amenities are also provided in each chalet, as are light snacks. Meals are served for the adults at either the lodge dining room or around the open-air boma. Children under 8 have special meal times (earlier than the adults meal times), with food more suited to young palates. Mark's Camp is the only lodge to be fenced to keep predators at bay – wildlife at Lalibela is free to roam throughout the reserve.

Child-friendly Family Rates

Children under the age of 12 pay 50% of the adult rate. This rate includes accommodation, all meals, game drives as applicable, children's activities as described and any child-minding or baby-sitting during the above times. For bookings visit www.lalibela.net

About the Author: Vernon Wait is an owner of Pembury Tours - a leading SATSA accredited tour operator established in 1996, offering tour itineraries across Southern and Eastern Africa. For more information visit www.pemburytours.com

*Generation-Z is generally defined as a collective cohort born after the year 2000 (the children of Generation-X and / or Millennials). Source: Wikipedia.

Chilly Powder
in the
FRENCH ALPS

Chilly Powder is an appropriate name for a 4-star ski hotel located in the famous Portes du Soleil, where snow is almost guaranteed and average normal winter temperatures range around -1.6°C.

Based in the heart of the famous Portes du Soleil hamlet of Prodains in the French ski resort of Morzine, Avoriaz, Chilly Powder boasts a true ski-to-door experience, with a high-speed gondola to Avoriaz located near the main hotel entrance. This means that guests have the advantage of not needing transportation each day before they even start to ski. They also have a free button lift 30 meters away, a great way to get your ski legs warmed up on your arrival.

The area has plenty to offer for skiers of all abilities and ages, with over 650km of skiable terrain on the doorstep. Morzine is also the ideal place to discover two cultures as the resort lies in the heart of the Franco-Swiss region of the Portes du Soleil and its 12 interconnected resorts - meaning you can ski across the border into Switzerland, with views of Mont Blanc in one direction and Lake Geneva in the other. Portes du Soleil is among the largest ski areas in the world. A 1,950 meter-high pass that connects Morgins to Les Crosets.

The four-star chalet business, rated number one on Trip Advisor in the region, was founded by British couple Paul and Francesca Eyre who say: "We built Chilly Powder from the ground up almost 20 years ago now. It is so much more than just a hotel, it's also our family home, and we put our hearts and souls into creating a memorable, unrivalled experience for every single one of our guests".

Being a family run business means the couple have thought of every little detail to accommodate even the youngest of skiers at the chalet. Each winter, Chilly Powder's fully qualified nannies care for children as young as 3 months old, allowing parents to enjoy their time on the mountain whilst knowing their children are well cared for and entertained in their in-house crèche. From age 4, Chilly Powder children can join their private ski school, with up to 6 children in each class.

Within the main hotel, "Au Coin Du Feu" (meaning by the fireside), rooms are individually themed and guests can book to stay in The Garden Room, Toy Room, English Room, Safari Suite or Music room amongst many others. Smaller catered chalets "Des Amis" (sleeping up to 9) and "Plan Des Rochers" (sleeping up to 14) are just a few steps away from the main hotel or there are the self-catered options in "Chalet Trembles" (sleeping up to 16) or "Chalet L'Ancetre" (sleeping up to 9).

Over the years, Chilly Powder has become renowned for its exquisite food and bespoke service, with their head chef creating all his menus using fresh and local produce, aided by owner Francesca who is a Cordon Bleu chef. Francesca says: "We love to provide our guests with

a wow factor that excites them and is completely different to other ski/ chalet companies. We cater for all tastes and provide restaurant quality meals. Our menu is one of the main reasons why our guests come back year after year."

Chilly Powder is also perfectly equipped for non-skiers or anyone looking to take a break from the slopes, with the chalet-hotel also providing direct access to a range of activities, including ice sleigh rides, glacier walking and ice diving in the winter, and white water rafting, hydro speeding, paragliding and trail running in the summer.

The ski to the door location, family friendly atmosphere, superb cuisine and excellent facilities make Chilly Powder entirely unique in Morzine if not the Alps and keep guests coming back year on year.

For more information visit www.chillypowder.com

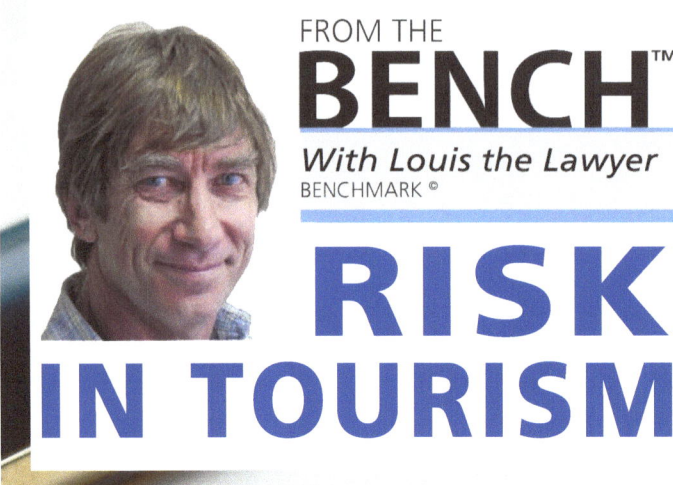

FROM THE

BENCH™

With Louis the Lawyer
BENCHMARK ©

RISK IN TOURISM

THE LAW: CONTRACTS

- Part 23 -

Enforcing Your Contract: Homework – What To Do Before You Go Ahead

THE NEXT STEP I.E. STEP 4 IS TO CONSIDER WHO TO CONSULT (REFRESHER: STEP 1 WAS/HOW ENFORCEABLE IS YOUR CONTRACT; STEP 2 WAS/HAVE THE REQUISITES BEEN MET; STEP 3 THE IMPACT]

In Part 23 we discussed the various parties that litigation would impact upon. Let's now consider the parties you should consult in the process of deciding whether or not you should proceed with litigation, which decision must be taken at management (Board, if applicable) level.

The first must be legal but before your proceed in that regard, you MUST advise your insurer IMMEDIATELY, especially if you are not suing but being sued – the minute you receive a letter of demand or a summons is served upon your business, your policy requires you to advice your insurer forthwith, failing which you may void your policy! Furthermore they may well supervise or manage the entire process discussed below as they usually have their own preferred (external) 'legal team', although will or should still work hand-in-hand with your internal legal advisor.

The next must be legal. This will mean different things to different businesses as some will have an in-house legal advisor and others not. Such a person will have an intimate knowledge of more than just legal issues and will apply all the different disciplines and consult all the separate operations in arriving at a final decision as it is imperative not make such a decision in isolation. As such a person is a salaried employee, it may lead to a material cost saving as practising attorneys (solicitors) and advocates (barristers) will demand a substantial deposit.

Once such an internal decision has been made or if the business does not employ a legal advisor or have an internal advisor, the next step would be to consult with external attorneys and they may well suggest appointing an advocate (Counsel), which in turn may requiring the appointment of a senior (long standing) advocate and a junior.

You can well imagine the fees so I strongly advise that you request these parties to provide you with the following: advice on evidence (be it documentary requirements or which persons or experts to call as witnesses) and advice on the merits (effectively your chances of success). The latter may well be positive but if some of the crucial evidence (a document may be missing or you may not be able to trace/get hold of a key witness) is not available, you may well reconsider proceeding – it is like having a first class rifle with poor ammunition! Times have changed and if the outcome of both these enquiries are positive, don't feel shy to ask for a fee estimate!

Once you've decided to proceed and have a fee estimate, engage your finance department about available funds. Such a discussion must not only focus on the legal fees but also travel and accommodation costs and the fees of experts that may have to be summoned.

Once the above is done and dusted, if not simultaneously, engage with your marketing and/or PR department/firm – as discussed in an earlier part of this series on contracts, brand management is crucial so you want to pre-empt the rumour mongering/grapevine ASAP. I know of such firms who have various template responses ready so that press releases can be dealt with promptly.

Finally consulting with your human resources regarding such matters as internal communications and staff leave i.e. current or future applications for leave of employees who may be called as witnesses.

To be continued in Part 24.

This series of articles explores the legal aspects associated with the risks of operating an adventure tourism business, with specific relevance to the legal framework applicable to South Africa.

Part 1 can be read online HERE, Part 2 HERE, Part 3 HERE, and Part 4 HERE.

Part 5

By 'Louis The Lawyer'

Image courtesy of Canopy Tours

ADVENTURE TOURISM
from a legal perspective

Summary

Part 1 provided definitions for the term Adventure, while Part 2 looked at risk in terms of Nationality of Participant, Service Providers, Bookings, and Terms & Conditions, and Part 3 covered Indemnity and Requirements of the CPA, and Part 4 covered risk identificer signage must be used/go in hand with a sound indemnity and waiver form.

DUTY OF CARE

Negligence

Negligence can be broadly defined as conduct which involves unreasonable risk of harm to others OR the failure to exercise the degree of care which the circumstances demand. The latter definition brings into the fold the concept of duty of care: the duty to avoid doing something or to do something that may reasonably and probably cause harm to those to whom the duty is owed linked to a subsequent breach of that duty.

There are various circumstances as well as contracts and statutes (laws or enactments of parliament or local government) that can give rise to or impose a duty to take care.

Omission

Let's start by considering whether and how an omission (i.e. the failure to act) can give rise to such a duty. It is said that *'a mere omission'* does not give rise to such a duty as opposed to an omission in the process of performing a positive act: e.g. when making a booking but failing to advise the pax of imminent danger – there is in my view no difference whether the intended journey is of a local or international nature.

It is therefore imperative that the service provider (This includes the entire supply chain from e.g. the tour operator to all third parties supplying products or services) must be familiar with the client and his/her particular needs as well as the destination(s) and the route thereto/from as well as the credentials of all third parties providing service and products.

The willy nilly appointment of such third parties without thoroughly vetting them and their products (A due diligence is recommended) may well result itself being amounting to such an omission and thus give rise to liability. The CPA stresses the exposure of the entire supply chain and even in the case of section 61 absolute/no fault product liability can be apportioned.

Relationship

The relationship between the parties may give rise to such a duty. One may well argue that the travel agent or tour operator owes all pax such a duty. It is therefore important to act within the scope of your professional training, skills & related knowledge. So given that travel agents and tour operators are or should be properly trained and have the skills and knowledge (see above) but fails to impart that knowledge and/or apply such skills and training, the court may well find that they had a duty of care, breached same and will be held liable for the consequences. This exposure is extended to employees (acting in the course and scope of their duties) so it is important to have and apply a thorough travel policy. An area of concern in this regard is how to deal with employees going on a so-called *'frolic of their own'* when away on a business trip!

It is the breach of the above duties of care or such as may be demanded by the circumstances that gives rise to negligence, provided such breach involves an *'unreasonable risk of harm to others'*, which may well be the case if applied to the circumstances sketched/envisaged.

However the courts are not unreasonable and when applying the so-called foreseeability test, i.e. the extent to which the occurrence should have been anticipated, it will look not only at the possibility of the incident occurring, but also the remoteness of such an occurrence; whether or not, even if it were to occur, the nature of the harm (serious or negligible) was such as a nature that the mythical 'reasonable man' would have guarded against it – the latter would mean an assessment of the steps taken/that could have been taken and the efficacy thereof. t

To be continued in Part 6.

By **Mary Smith**.

HOTEL TECHNOLOGY TRENDS
— You Need to Know —

Review Widget/Plugin Implementation

- Embedding a review widget or plugin on you website allows **potential guests to read unbiased feedback** from your previous guests without leaving your website.

- Sites like **TripAdvisor** offer free widgets / plugins.

- As widgets / plugins **automatically take content from other sites** where a **potentially negative review** may be posted, it would also feature this review on your website.

- Some **hoteliers** may be slow to implement these widgets because of this.

- However reviews are an opportunity for hotels to **improve their customer service**.

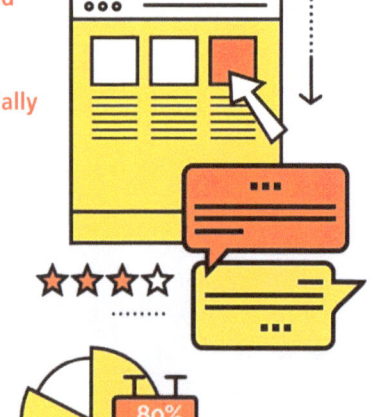

 **How Do They Improve Customer Service?**

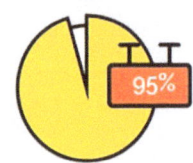 95%

 60%

80%

95% of online shoppers suspect that reviewers may have been censored if they do not see any negative reviews.

More than 60% of TripAdvisor users say that a good management response to a negative review makes them more likely to book, compared to no response.

80% of TripAdvisor users say they think a hotel cares more when it posts management responses.

 **Key Takeaway:** Implement review widgets/plugins to perfect customer service and manage your hotel's online reputation.

Source: *GuestRevu 2016*.

Social Media Cultivation

Except for **Facebook**, no other **social media channel** is used intensively across the hotel industry. Only 1 in 3 currently have **videos on YouTube**, even though video has become the single most important online format predicted to account for **80% of global internet traffic by 2019**.

 Social Media Usage in the Hotel Industry

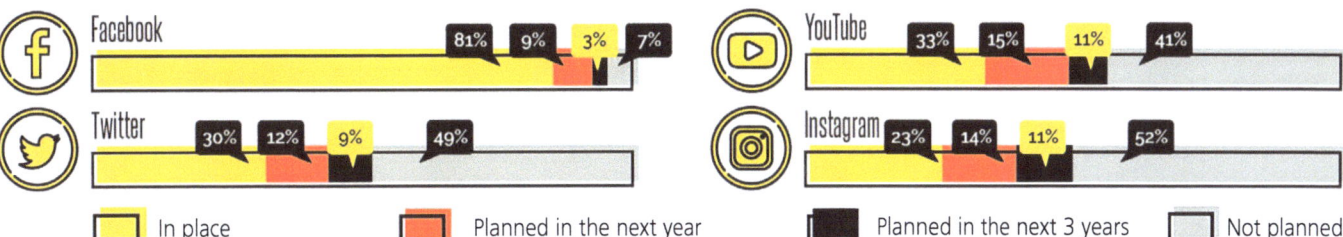

	In place	Planned in the next year	Planned in the next 3 years	Not planned
Facebook	81%	9%	3%	7%
YouTube	33%	15%	11%	41%
Twitter	30%	12%	9%	49%
Instagram	23%	14%	11%	52%

Key Takeaway: Utilise social media more, especially video based channels like YouTube to future proof your hotel online marketing efforts.

Source: *Hotel Industry 4.0 Study, OHV & Roland Berger, 2016 & Hootsuite.*

The Future Could Be 5G

5G is the latest variation of mobile. It is not expected for mass adoption before **2020**.

3D Image Exploration

 In a 5G enabled hotel, potential guests may be able to choose their hotel room stay by viewing & exploring the hotel in 3D images.

This could be similar to Google's Streetview & gives guests a virtual tour.

Self-Check-In

 5G mobile could lead to extremely efficient 'self-check-in' options for guests.

 This could see front of house hotel staff evolving into guest service co-ordinator roles and communicating using mobile social media & apps.

Staff Training

 Mobile learning could provide real time on the job training using software to analyse, rate and provide advice on how to improve employees' service skills.

 5G mobile could also prove invaluable for staff selection & training.

 It is early days yet, but keep an eye on the rise of 5G technology in the next 4 years and start a conversation around it now with hotel management.

Source: *eHotelier, 2016.*

 **About the Author: Mary Smith** work on the digital marketing for Ard na Sidhe Country House in Co. Kerry, Ireland. ardnasidhe.com

HUAWEI Launches
Mate 9

Unveiled in Munich, Germany on November 3rd, Huawei Consumer Business Group presented two of the most anticipated devices of the year – the Huawei Mate 9 and the exclusive Porsche Design Huawei Mate 9.

Building on Huawei's success in delivering beautifully-designed, powerful mobile devices, the newest members of the Mate Series provides users with an all new Android experience – featuring the Kirin 960 for the fastest computing performance, SuperCharge technology and a stunning new UX.

The HUAWEI Mate 9 features a dynamic interplay of industry-leading hardware and advanced software that work together to keep users a step ahead. Key features include:
• Kirin 960 chipset, the world's highest performing smartphone processor*;
• EMUI 5.0, an intuitive user interface that streamlines the users' experience with the OS SuperCharge technology that delivers a full day's charge in 20 minutes;
• Second generation Leica dual-lens camera with 12-megapixel RGB sensor, 20-megapixel monochrome sensor and Hybrid Zoom, featuring a superior 2x magnification;
•Maximized Performance and Speed with Kirin 960.

With over 100 million units sold, Huawei's Kirin chipsets showcase the company's deep understanding of the kind of power and experience users are looking for – a fast mobile device that is intuitive and reliable. The Kirin 960 is the world's first chipset to feature an ARM Cortex-A73/A53 Octa-core CPU and Mali G71 Octa-core GPU, to deliver the best multi-core performance among all smartphone SoCs, while reducing power consumption by 15 percent.

A Safe, Faster-Charging Battery

The HUAWEI Mate 9 combines a 4000 mAh high-density battery with Huawei's all new SuperCharge technology to increase battery life and provide over two days of uninterrupted performance. This includes a 40 percent increase in CDMA call time and a 20 percent increase in gaming time.

Supporting 5A fast charging, SuperCharge technology enables a 50 percent improvement over the previous generation – 10 minutes of charge provides enough power to watch two full movies. Most importantly, the battery sets a new standard in charging technology including Super Safe 5-gate protection, which offers real-time voltage, current and temperature monitoring to eliminate safety hazards and safeguard battery life.

Professional-quality Smartphone Photography

Following the incredible success of the Huawei P9, the HUAWEI Mate 9 dual-lens camera, co-engineered with Leica, now includes a 12-megapixel/F2.2 RGB sensor, a 20-megapixel/F2.2 monochrome sensor and enhanced image fusion algorithms that work in concert to produce stunning photography. The RGB sensor captures true-to-life colors, while the monochrome sensor captures intricate details and depth resulting in the iconic Leica Image Style. When paired with the leading dual-lens camera Optical Image Stabilization (OIS) solution and the industry's first dual-camera pixel binning technology, the HUAWEI Mate 9 has a superior night shot capability.

Performance in Design

The HUAWEI Mate 9 builds upon the Mate Series' highly-regarded design DNA and uses the finest materials to deliver a smartphone that features a 5.9" FHD display and is both beautifully designed and comfortable to use. The casing is constructed using 50 unique processes including one hour of CNC milling, resulting in a high-precision unibody metal frame. Every detail – from the soft sandblasted texture to the gorgeous color palette – is a result of more than 25 years' experience in delivering refined craftsmanship.

Design Icon Meets Technology Leader

The PORSCHE DESIGN HUAWEI Mate 9 is a limited edition smartphone combining Porsche Design's signature brand aesthetic with Huawei's mobile engineering expertise. Together Huawei and Porsche Design have achieved a new pinnacle where Porsche Design's unique signature aesthetic meets Huawei's market-leading technology. With the PORSCHE DESIGN HUAWEI Mate 9, Huawei introduces a remarkable 5.5" curved AMOLED display that offers a smooth, sleek feel. It will be available exclusively in Graphite Black.

For more information visit http://consumer.huawei.com

Geekbench 4.0.0 multi-core CPU performance and DDR performance.

www.ingramcontent.com/pod-product-compliance
Lightning Source LLC
Chambersburg PA
CBHW050410180526
45159CB00005B/2218